This  belongs to.

For more kindergarten writing paper, please visit the above page.

For other notebooks to help organize and enjoy your life, please visit the above page.

Kindergarten Writing Paper with Lines for Kids

Jett Express Learning Publications
https://www.amazon.com/Jett-Express-Learning -Publications/e/B08ZPWRQ45?ref_=dbs_p_pbk _r00_abau_000000

ASIN: B08Y4HBFFX

JEllēB Press
https://www.amazon.com/JEll%C4%93B-Press/e/B0 8ZNR386T?ref_=dbs_p_pbk_r00_abau_000000

Thank you for supporting our small business!

Made in the USA
Las Vegas, NV
23 May 2021